TOTALLY AMAZING
Animals

TWO CAN™

LONDON ■ PRINCETON

Published by Two-Can Publishing
43-45 Dorset Street, London W1U 7NA

© 2001 Two-Can Publishing

For information on Two-Can books and multimedia,
call (0)20 7224 2440, fax (0)20 7224 7005, or visit our web site at
http://www.two-canpublishing.com

RAINFORESTS

Author: Kate Graham; Consultant: Jonathan Elphick; Illustrations: Woody, Lorna Kent.

SEA CREATURES

Author: Iqbal Hussain; Consultant: Dr Frances Dipper; Illustrations: Andrew Peters.

NIGHT ANIMALS

Author: Iqbal Hussain; Consultant: Gary Boller; Illustrations: Jonathan Elphick.

PB ISBN 1-85434-771-3

Paperback 10 9 8 7 6 5 4 3 2 1

A catalogue record for this book is available from the British Library.

Photographs: pp.7, 8/9, 42/43, 69 (top): Robert Harding Picture Library; pp.10, 29, 45, 54, 63, 78/79:
Tony Stone Images; pp.11, 15, 21, 26/27, 32, 67, 85, 86/87: Bruce Coleman Ltd; pp.12/13: Still Pictures;
pp.13, 77: FLPA; pp.16, 31, 37, 39 (top & bottom right), 46/47, 50 (left), 55, 57, 58/59, 62, 72, 81:
Planet Earth Pictures; pp.18/19, 25, 30, 71, 83, 84: National History Photographic Agency;
p.20: Premaphotos Wildlife; pp.22/23: Michael & Patricia Fogden; p.33: The Natural History Museum, London;
pp. 38/39, 60/61: The Stock Market; pp.40/41, 50/51, 75, 82, 86, 92: Oxford Scientific Films;
p.49: Powerstock; pp.52/53: Ardea London Ltd; p.61: BBC Natural History Unit Picture Library; p.69 (bottom):
Science Photo Library; p.73: Minden Pictures; p.76: Powerstock/Zefa; p.89: Telegraph Colour Library;
p.90: Fogden Natural History Photographs; p.91: Hammer Film Productions, courtesy of the Kobal Collection;
p.93: Images Colour Library.
Every effort has been made to contact the copyright owner of the image of the tarsier monkey reproduced on pages 68/69.
Two-Can hopes to be able to correct this omission in future editions of the book.

Printed in Hong Kong by Wing King Tong

Contents

Rainforests

Contents

Tricky words are explained on page 94.

Journey into the Jungle

Are you ready to join an expedition into the amazing world of the steaming-hot rainforest, where it rains nearly every day? Trees tower high in the sky and amazing animals live everywhere — from the tops of the trees to their tangled roots.

That's weird

There are so many different kinds of rainforest animals that scientists haven't given them all names yet.

What's your name?

Where in the world?

Rainforests don't grow just anywhere. They are found in the hottest places in the world. These hot spots all lie near the equator, which is an imaginary line that goes round the middle of the Earth.

Leafy layers

A rainforest is divided into three layers. The leafy layer at the top of the trees is called the canopy. Below the canopy, smaller plants grow in the understorey. The forest floor is damp, dark and a bit spooky!

Giant trees peep out above the canopy.

Monkeys swing and birds fly in the canopy.

Frogs hop and snakes slither in the understorey.

Jaguars prowl and insects march on the forest floor.

▲ Each kind of animal has its own favourite spot in a particular layer of the rainforest.

GREEN & GORGEOUS

Record breaker

The prize for the biggest flower goes to the giant rafflesia that grows on the forest floor in parts of Asia. It can be as wide as you are tall, but it's no beauty. It has thick warty petals and a spiky centre that stinks of rotting meat. The horrible whiff attracts swarms of flies.

The bubble gum you blow into bubbles is made from chicle, which comes from sapodilla trees in the Amazon rainforest.

That's weird

Male bees flock to the bucket orchid to gather a gooey mess that will impress female bees. The male rubs it on his legs, then flies off in search of a hot date!

Rubber starts off as a milky juice which flows from a rubber tree. But it ends up as bouncy, stretchy material, perfect for making all kinds of things, from footballs and bicycle tyres to wet suits.

Yumm!

Feeling fruity

The durian is the smelliest fruit in the rainforest. Its stench of rotten fish drifts up to nearly one kilometre away. When the durian is ripe, animals sniff it out then feast on the stinky fruit. Many people think that the durian tastes delicious, too.

11

Rainforest animals have plenty to talk about. Frogs croak, monkeys whoop and birds screech, which is their way of saying 'Hi!' to friends and 'Get lost' to enemies.

Animal chatters

Strange but true

The tiny poison dart frog is just over one centimetre long. That's the size of a small grape.

How much louder do I have to be?

Frog chorus

All kinds of male frogs serenade female frogs with deep throaty croaks. The male with the loudest booming croak wins the affection of the female. Frogs also croak to tell enemies to hop off!

Crrroak!

▲ This frog can stretch the skin under its chin like a balloon to make a mega-loud croak!

A nose for noise

The male proboscis monkey has a long droopy growth for his nose, which he 'plays' loudly like a trumpet. He lets other monkeys in his group know that he's boss by warning them of danger and calling them together for meetings.

Tuneful gibbons

Gibbons are musical animals. When male and female gibbons mate, they stay friends forever and sing duets to one another. A family of gibbons also calls across the canopy to keep other families away from its patch.

13

Rainforest animals have some strange ideas about setting up a home and starting a family. Most leave their young to look after themselves, but a few take great care of their babies.

Forest families

BACHELOR BIRD HOUSE

The male bower bird makes a fancy house with matching flowers and feathers to attract a female bird.

This spot is just perfect.

Then he adds a splash of colour with berry juice.

SQUASHED BERRIES

I like this shade of blue.

When the house is ready, he waits inside for a female bower bird.

Cool place to live!

Well, hello!

Strange but true

Chimpanzees live in close-knit families. They groom each other's fur, hold hands and even kiss each other!

Gorilla picnic

Each morning, the father gorilla, called the silverback, wakes up the family to enjoy a meal of fruit, leaves and bark. After breakfast, the grown-ups snooze while the young play games. The young gorillas will stay with their parents until they are more than ten years old.

▼ A mother sloth hangs upside down from a tree by her toes. Her baby holds on tight.

I'm just hanging around.

Lazy baby

There's no pressure on a baby sloth to leave home. Each long-haired sloth baby spends six to nine months hanging on to the fur on its mother's stomach. Then the lazy-bones moves off on its own, extremely slowly, to find its own tree, where it may live for years and years.

Hey, Dad just swallowed the kids!

Being a dad is a serious business for the male Darwin's frog. When the eggs hatch into tadpoles, he scoops them up and carries them around in a pouch in his mouth. After about three weeks, the proud dad spits out the little froglets, who can now hop around by themselves!

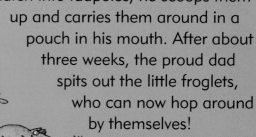

Fruits of the forest

What's on the menu in the rainforest? Many animals like to gobble up crunchy insects and other scrumptious creatures. But there are also plenty of vegetarians who munch only leaves, shoots, fruit and nuts.

Strange but true

A gorilla treats itself to breakfast in bed. It just lies back in its grass nest and picks fresh green leaves from nearby.

▲ A gorilla has a massive appetite. Every day, this vegetarian spends six hours eating.

Jaw-some!

An agouti is a champion nut-cracker that has incredibly strong jaws. It is one of the few animals that can crack the tough Brazil nut. The agouti is similar to other rodents because it buries a hoard of nuts to save for later. But the forgetful creature can't always remember where it put them! The lost nuts often sprout up later and grow into trees.

HOME-GROWN LUNCH

Leaf-cutter ants work in teams to grow food. One team collects leaves.

Another team chews the leaves until they turn into a sticky pulp.

Tasty fungus grows on the pulp. The ants all feast on the fungus.

Cats go fishing

Jaguars are the only big cats that live in Central and South America. Unlike many cats, jaguars are happy in water and are strong swimmers. They enjoy eating fish and sometimes even catch crocodiles. They also eat smaller mammals. Jaguars are good climbers and often hide in leafy trees, waiting for their next meal to stroll by. Then they jump down and give their victim a nasty surprise.

That's weird

Most insects eat plants, but with the pitcher plant it's the other way round. An insect slides from the rim of the plant into a pool of liquid and drowns. Then the pitcher plant digests it.

Gotcha!

▲ A chameleon glues a victim to its long tongue with a sticky glob of spit! Yuck!

Crafty chameleon

SNACK ATTACK

In a fraction of a second, the quick-draw chameleon snaps up a tasty insect. The chameleon's tongue is as long as its body!

A chameleon's tongue ▶ can be this super-long!

0 cm 1 2 3 4 5 6 7

0 inches 1 2

Rainbow reptile

Imagine being able to change colour! In minutes, a chameleon turns from one colour to another to blend in with its surroundings and to hide from enemies. It also changes colour with its mood. An angry chameleon comes out in orange patches to let other chameleons know that it's cross.

For my final trick!

When all else fails, the chameleon has one last trick to fool enemies. It plays dead. When face to face with danger, it flops to one side, with a limp body, drooping eyelids and stiff legs. As soon as its enemy turns its back, the chameleon makes a dash for it.

Did that twig just move? Did that leaf just fly away? Rainforest animals are masters of disguise. They have all kinds of tricks to help them catch dinner and to avoid being eaten themselves!

That's weird

An orchid mantis is patient and cunning. It looks just like an orchid gently swaying in the breeze. When an insect lands nearby, it pounces.

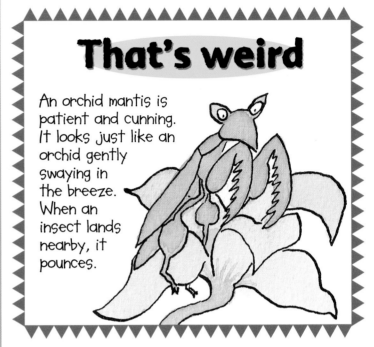

Bottoms up!

When this eyespot frog feels threatened, it shows its attacker an eyeful of the black circles on its bottom. The frightened attacker backs off because it thinks that the circles are the eyes of a much larger creature!

Vanishing act

The ornate orb-weaver spider flattens itself against the bark of a tree, stays absolutely still and – hey, presto – it seems to disappear. The spider's colouring exactly matches the mouldy, flaky and mottled colours of the bark.

camouflage

Strange but true

A gecko can't blink so it uses its tongue to wash its eyes.

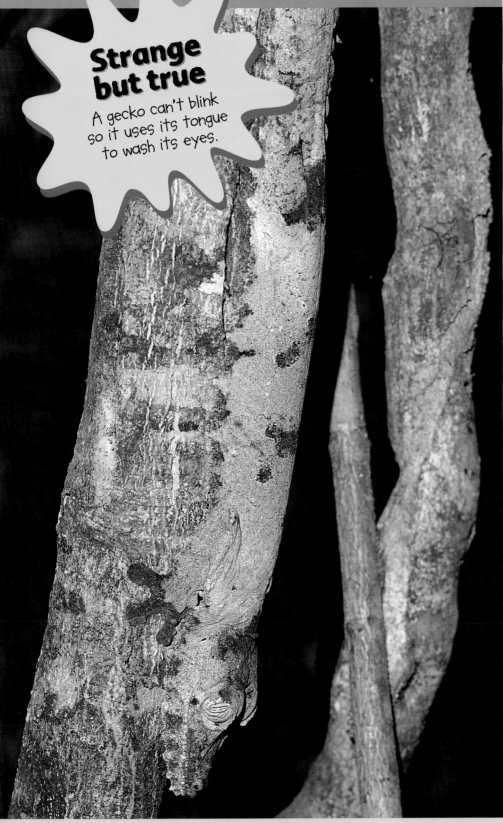

The spiky thorn bug looks just like a genuine prickly plant thorn, so most enemies leave it alone.

The walking-stick insect is an experienced actor. It blends in with its surroundings and, if necessary, won't move for up to six hours!

▲ Look closely. Can you make out the bulging eyes of the gecko lizard? Its patchy green and brown skin looks just like bark.

21

Danger!
Red alert

There are always watchful predators about, ready to fight to the death. Many have ingenious ways of catching their prey. They may trap, poison, bite or even strangle it. Or they may just swallow it up alive.

Strange but true

Snakes can stretch their elastic skin to help them swallow their prey.

That's weird

An ogre-faced spider weaves a web about the size of a postage stamp and waits in ambush. When an insect zooms by, it covers it with the sticky net and delivers a lethal bite.

Viper swipe!

The eyelash viper fixes its eyes on its target, rotates its fangs at the front of its upper jaw into position, aims, then bites with deadly accuracy. It injects lethal poison straight through its fangs into the prey.

Flying killers

An eagle is the biggest and fastest flying killing machine in the rainforest. It can spy a monkey in the canopy from more than three kilometres above, swoop down at lightning speed and snatch it with its razor-sharp talons. Then it flies away to enjoy its meal in peace.

Dinner-time!

Stranglehold

The anaconda is a giant snake that can grow as long as six children lying end to end. It wraps its long body round and round its victim, then squeezes tight. The victim can't escape and soon chokes to death.

▲ In double-quick time, the tiny eyelash viper's head darts forwards to grab a passing lizard in its big mouth.

Lethal mini-beasts

Many of the deadliest killers in the forest are also the smallest. Insects and spiders are top-notch hunters that catch their prey in all kinds of disagreeable ways.

Strong stink!

The rove beetle has a smart but smelly disguise. It looks like a piece of dung! It hangs around real dung, where it gobbles up flies which are drawn to the honking stuff. And when there's no dung around, the beetle makes its own stink to lure flies to their doom.

Believe it or not

Some insects use chemical warfare by spraying enemies with blistering liquid.

Slurping spiders

A black widow spider is enemy number one to insects. Its venom can be 15 times more deadly than that of a rattlesnake. One small nip from a black widow's needle-sharp fangs and it's all over for an insect. Then the spider sucks out the insect's insides for a tasty treat.

WASP VERSUS TARANTULA

The female hawk wasp is a small but daring opponent of the tarantula spider. She dives in bravely.

I must avoid those fearsome fangs!

The wasp injects venom into the spider so that it cannot move, but is still alive. Then...

Ouch! You bully!

...she drags the spider to her nest and lays eggs on it. When the eggs hatch, the baby wasps eat the spider.

Phew! Winning is hard work!

24

▼ The praying mantis claps together her two front legs to grip her unfortunate victim.

Munching mantis

The female praying mantis is a calm and calculating killer. She sits extremely still, holding up her front legs as if saying a prayer. But this devious insect is really waiting for a tasty morsel to fly by. The praying mantis is so greedy that she sometimes gobbles up her partner after mating!

What's in a name?

Battalions of army ants march like real soldiers in search of food. They are fierce hunters that capture and kill.

Batty bats

Bats are amazing. They are mammals, like you, but they can fly. When these acrobats of the air pause for rest, they nest together in big groups.

▲ During the day, tent bats snuggle up together, resting in preparation for night flights when they search for fruit and insects.

Tree-houses

Tent bats camp out in the understorey near fruit trees. The bats make cosy, hanging tents from large leaves. First the little nibblers bite small holes along either side of the leaf. This bends the leaf to make a roof shape. Then they hook their feet into the holes and hang, heads down, safe from the heat of the sun and out of the wet of the rain.

This is cosy!

Life's a breeze...
swinging in the trees

The canopy is full of animal acrobats and trapeze artists. Monkeys, frogs and snakes leap from tree to tree with incredible ease. They seem to fly through the air — bobbing and tumbling, but never losing their balance.

FLYING SSSSNAKES

Where's that frog going?

It curves itself in an S-shape and soars through the air. The chase is on.

I'm behind you!

A slippery snake slithers and wriggles, then jumps after its prey.

It lands safely on a branch. Gulp!

Branching out

Monkeys are graceful tree acrobats. They stretch and swing, gripping on to branches with their strong hands and feet. An orangutan can soar huge distances between one branch and the next. But a big, old male orangutan is too heavy to live in the trees, so he retires to the ground and moves on all fours.

28

▲ An orangutan has much longer arms than legs!

Super glue

Tree frogs have real suction power. Their special fingers and toes stick to slippery tree trunks and branches. They are so sure-footed, they can hang upside-down from a branch without falling off.

Going up

Scientists who study animals in the rainforest need a head for heights. They use climbing ropes, walkways and even hot-air balloons to make sure they get a bird's-eye view of what's going on in the treetops.

Squawk!

In the swim

Huge rivers, such as the mighty Amazon, flow through every rainforest. If you take a peek below the surface of these murky waters, you'll see some creatures that are wonderfully weird!

It's shocking!

An electric eel's muscles work like batteries. They make electric signals, which help the eel to find its way around the muddy river and stun its prey. It can zap its victims with up to 650 volts – enough electric power to stun a horse!

I like my fish fried!

Believe it or not

A crocodile has a pair of see-through eyelids that protect its eyes while they are still open.

Open wide

A crocodile's huge jaws and sharp teeth would scare any dentist. This ferocious reptile lurks with only its eyes and nostrils above the water, waiting for a thirsty animal to come for a drink. SNAP! It opens its huge jaws and the unfortunate creature is dragged under the surface to a grisly death.

What's in a name?

The mudskipper jumps and skips along the muddy shores on strong pectoral fins. It's just as happy living underwater, too.

Gentle giant

What eats a vast amount of plants each day and looks like a swimming elephant? The manatee. It's the largest rainforest animal and scientists think that it really is a distant relative of the elephant. It swims slowly using its flippers and tears at plants with its long lip.

Under the microscope

The piranha fish has rows of needle-sharp teeth. It smells the blood of an injured animal, chases it, then rips it up!

▲ A manatee knocks sand off a plant with its amazingly long lip and then swallows it whole.

HA HA! How do electric eels get to school? They take a buzz. HEE HEE!

Prize day

It's prize day in the rainforest and you have a chance to meet even more amazing plants and animals. Some are huge and some are tiny, but every one's a winner!

Fearsome froggy

The prize for the scariest animal goes to the poison dart frog. It looks harmless, but this frog is one of the deadliest creatures around. Some have enough poison in their skin to kill 50 snakes.

What a mouthful

The goliath bird-eating tarantula beats all other spiders for size. Measuring as much as 28 centimetres from toe to toe, this hairy bird-eater fits nicely across a large dinner plate. Imagine finding this giant spider on the table instead of your lunch. Eek!

Beetle that

The gold medal for weightlifting goes to the rhinoceros beetle. This colossal creepy-crawly is so strong, it simply lifts up other insects that get in its way, using its pointed horns.

Wonder wings

You can hardly miss the Queen Alexandra's birdwing in a butterfly parade. The female's wings can measure an incredible 28 centimetres from tip to tip, making it the largest butterfly in the world.

actual size

Teeny weeny

Here's a bird that's a champion featherweight! The tiny bee hummingbird of Cuba weighs in at a record-breaking 1.4 grams, which is too light even to register on a kitchen scale. This tiny tweeter is also a star gymnast. It can fly backwards, sideways and upside down, or just hover on the spot.

Creepy climbers

Rattan plants from Southeast Asia are at the top of the class for climbing. They grow along the ground and crawl up tree trunks, stretching to a height of more than 152 metres. That's one and a half times taller than the Statue of Liberty!

TOTALLY AMAZING

Sea Creatures

Contents

Tricky words are explained on page 94.

Splashdown...
...into a watery world

Nearly three-quarters of our world is covered by oceans and seas. Creatures of every shape and size live here — from tiny, invisible plankton to blue whales, which are the biggest animals on Earth.

That's weird

Until recently, no one really knew what lurked beneath the waves. Centuries ago, sailors thought that the ocean was full of giant sea monsters.

Which way home?

Most sea creatures stick to their own patch of the ocean, where the temperature of the water suits them. Blue whales are at home in icy waters, but green sea turtles feel the cold so they prefer warm seas. Parrotfish swim in shallow water near coral reefs. Anglerfish stick to deep, dark trenches.

Exploring the deep

Today, scientists travel across the ocean floor in submersibles to explore sandy sea beds, spooky caves and rocky crags, packed full of amazing creatures. The submersibles carry cameras for studying the creatures in detail.

What are you staring at?

Believe it or not

A frogfish has joints on its fins. It can bend its fins just like you bend your elbows.

Come in — the water's great!

▲ Frogfish scramble over hard coral, looking for smaller fish to snap up.

On the mOve

Sea creatures move around in all sorts of strange ways. Some cut through the water with their sharp fins or bendy flippers. Others travel by squirting out water behind them. A few just float along, going where the sea takes them.

SAILFISH

Swimming champion

You wouldn't stand a chance in a race with a sailfish. This torpedo-shaped record breaker is the fastest swimmer in the ocean. It sails along at up to 108 kilometres per hour, faster than a cheetah runs on land.

▲ A sea turtle is like a powerful rowing machine. It pulls its body through the water with its oar-shaped flippers.

On the wing

A manta ray flies through the ocean like a mysterious, underwater bird. This gentle giant flaps its wing-like fins up and down to move. The fins measure up to eight metres across, which is as wide as a two-seater aeroplane.

Little squirts

A scallop swims by quickly opening and closing its hinged shell, just like a pair of clicking castanets. Jets of water shoot out from the shell's two halves and push the creature through the water.

Under the microscope

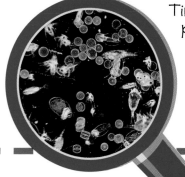

Tiny plankton are pushed along by powerful currents. They provide food for many creatures.

Hiking holiday

How would you like to take a long hike through deep waters? Once a year, crawfish trek for days across the ocean floor. Eels travel vast distances every year, too.

▲ Crawfish march across the ocean floor in a huge line of up to 50 creatures. Each crawfish stays in line by using the long, spiky feelers on its head to touch the tail of the crawfish in front.

Crawfish trek

Every autumn, violent storms batter the coast of Florida, USA, where crawfish live. To escape the terrible weather, the crawfish head for deeper waters. The adventurous trekkers file across plains where there are no hiding places. If an attacker strikes, the crawfish form a circle and wave their snapping pincers to scare off the enemy.

That's weird

Female eels swim over 6,400 kilometres from Europe to the Sargasso Sea, near Bermuda. At the end of this marathon journey, the courageous eels lay their eggs, before dying of exhaustion!

I'm sure we should have turned left ages ago.

Strange but true

Crawfish walk for up to a week, travelling both day and night.

Sea Sounds

Sea creatures send love messages, chat to their babies and even set off alarm signals. The ocean is a really noisy place!

Believe it or not

A blue whale can shout 500 times louder than you can.

Shrimp with a snap

Everyone knows when a pistol shrimp's in town. This creature fires off loud cracking noises to frighten its enemies. It snaps its claws together to make a sound like a gunshot and its enemies flee in fear.

▲ Dolphins make more than 30 different sounds, including furious clicks and whistles. They are champion underwater gossips!

WHISTLES AND CLICKS

SEA CREATURES SING LOVE SONGS AND SHOUT LOUDLY

A male toadfish sings the perfect love song by vibrating a small sac inside his body. A female toadfish finds the noise irresistible. She swims towards him, he grabs her with his mouth and they head off to mate.

Mum?

A female dugong constantly shouts at her baby. As they swim through fields of murky seagrass along the coast, the baby hears the sound loud and clear, and knows its mother is within reach.

A whale of a time

The prize for the ocean's biggest animal goes to the mighty whale. Baleen whales are gentle giants that filter tiny animals into their mouths through bony plates called baleen. Whales with teeth are fierce hunters that snap up fish and squid.

That's weird

A humpback whale is the opera singer of the deep. But listen too long and you'll get bored — the whale sings the same 30-minute song over and over again.

There she blows!

Just like you, a whale breathes air. It swims to the surface of the ocean and blows out a towering, misty spray through blowholes on the top of its head. Then it takes a few deep breaths and down it goes again. You won't find this creature ever gasping for breath.

Deep-sea battles

Try not to get into a fight with a sperm whale! This animal is the largest toothed whale in the ocean. Sperm whales have fierce underwater wrestling matches with giant squid. It's not always an easy battle, but the whale usually wins.

**Strange
but true**

Every now and then,
whales leap out of the water.
This is called breaching.
No one has any idea why
they do this.

▲ A humpback whale has incredibly long flippers which it holds out for balance when it jumps out
of the water. The humpback's young, known as calves, often shelter beneath these giant flippers.

Underwater garden

Beautiful gardens, called coral reefs, stretch across parts of the ocean floor. Tiny, dazzling fish dart through this fantastical world.

EXPLORING A REEF

▲ There are hundreds of different kinds of coral, from swaying fans and branches to brain-shaped coral!

Under the microscope

Coral looks like a plant but it is really made by the remains of these tiny sea animals called coral polyps.

Sworn enemies

The crown-of-thorns starfish is the coral reef's number one enemy. A hungry pack of these starfish can chomp through so much coral that they turn the reef into a dead zone.

BURP!!

Ocean families

Most sea creatures lay their eggs and swim off into the sunset. But a few proud parents stick around until their eggs hatch.

HOW A FLATFISH CHANGES FACES

When a baby flatfish is born, it looks like any other young fish, with an eye on each side of its head.

Hey, I look just like you!

As the flatfish grows older, its body becomes flatter. It lives on the sea bed with one eye stuck in the sand.

Mmm, everything's blurred now.

This eye travels round to join the other one. The fish sees better with both eyes on the same side of its head.

That's better.

You look weird!

Nanny patrol

After laying her eggs, a female lumpsucker leaves a male in charge. He keeps the eggs cool by fanning them frantically with his fin until they hatch. He also shoos away hungry crabs.

That's weird

A male sea horse has babies! A female lays hundreds of eggs in a pouch on his stomach and the proud dad carries them around until they hatch.

Operation turtle

Being a baby sea turtle is a dangerous business. The turtle hatches in the dead of night, then it makes a mad dash across the sand to the safety of the sea. On the way, pecking birds and hungry crabs may greedily gobble it up.

Beastly babes

Sand tiger sharks are fearsome fish, even before they are born. Unlike most sea creatures, tiger sharks do not hatch from eggs but grow inside their mother's body. As they grow, the bigger babies eat their smaller brothers and sisters. This ferocious family feast continues until only the two strongest tiger sharks are left.

Strange but true

Female turtles swim back to the sandy beaches where they were born to lay their eggs.

What's a baby shark's favourite treat? Jellyfish and icecream.

▲ Hatching from an egg can be hard work. Turtle eggs are buried deep beneath the sand, so the babies have to dig their way to the surface with their flippers.

Marine meals...

Sea creatures dine out in different ways. Some are roaming hunters, with sneaky methods of catching prey. Others just wait for a tasty treat to turn up.

Floating feast
Sea squirts have their food delivered. These swaying sea animals are rooted to the spot and wait for plankton to drift by. As sea squirts suck in water through a hole in their bodies, yummy plankton drift in too.

Bloodsucker
A hagfish is like a vampire. It attaches its sucker-like mouth to another fish. Then it grinds away at its victim's flesh with its horny teeth and feasts on the blood.

Safety in shoals

Swimming together in roving packs, called shoals, is one way to stay safe. Scientists think that small fish swim in huge shoals to make themselves look like one enormous fish. If the shoal is attacked, the fish scatter in all directions, confusing their enemy.

That's weird

Is it a bird? Is it a plane? No, it's a flying fish! When a flying fish is chased, it leaps out of the water and spreads out its fins to glide to safety.

Hey, come back here!

Ink-credible!

An octopus is like an ink pen. When it's attacked, it squirts out a vast cloud of black ink. While its attacker can't see a thing, the octopus makes a fast getaway.

I'll have that crab.

Crabs escape from hungry mouths by leaving bits of their bodies behind. When a crab is caught by its leg, the leg snaps off. A crab leg even has special weak points to help it break off more easily.

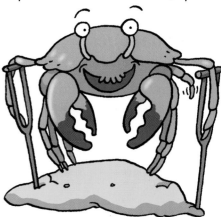

The crab quickly hobbles away. After a few months, the missing leg grows back, but it may be much smaller than the other ones. Still, it's a lucky escape!

The great Cover-up

Sea creatures are brilliant at putting on disguises. In seconds, they dress up or change colour to blend in with their surroundings. This camouflage stops them from being eaten by hungry predators.

Believe it or not

A butterflyfish wears false eyes on its tail to confuse its enemies.

All change

Flatfish, such as flounder and turbot, dress to suit the occasion. In minutes, they can turn from one colour to another to hide themselves. If you put a flatfish on a chessboard, it will even become checkered!

CRABBY CLOTHING

When a spider crab arrives at a beach, it gathers a pile of seaweed and designs a new set of clothes.

Uh oh! I'd better get changed.

The crab arranges the seaweed on its shell. Tiny spines on the crab's body hold it in place. Now it's almost invisible.

Where did that tasty-looking crab go?

When the crab moves on, it swaps its old clothes for a new outfit that is more suitable to its new surroundings.

I've always wanted a sponge suit.

▼ A stonefish is much more dangerous than it looks. Step on it and you'll be injected with a nasty poison!

Sinister stone

You need to be a hot-shot detective to discover a stonefish. This warty creature sits on the ocean floor, looking like a seaweed-covered rock that's been there for thousands of years. But the stonefish doesn't just sit there watching the watery world. When small fish swim by, it opens its mouth and greedily gobbles them up.

That's weird

A lionfish is one of the sea's biggest show-offs. Its dazzling stripes warn other fish that its spines are full of deadly poison!

Back off! I'm lethal.

Sticking together...

...perfect pals

Many sea creatures help each other out. These partnerships are often the best way for creatures to survive in this watery world.

▲ When a hermit crab moves out of its old shell, it takes along its partner, the sea anemone. The crab pulls the anemone off the old shell and gets it to attach itself to the new one.

Perfect protection

A sea anemone and a hermit crab are seasoned travellers. The anemone hitches a ride with the crab and protects it with its poisonous tentacles. In return, the anemone gets a ride across the ocean floor and stops for lunch on the way.

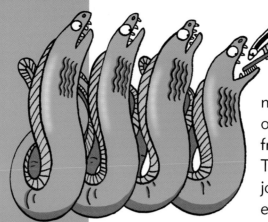

Wash and scrub

A cleaner wrasse offers a cleaning service for moray eels. The wrasse picks off dead skin and leftover food from between the eel's teeth. The wrasse is so good at its job that it often has several eager eels waiting in line.

That's weird

You won't find happier flatmates than a blind shrimp and a goby fish. The shrimp cleans the house while the goby keeps a look-out for unwelcome guests.

Air ambulance

Dolphin families are trained in first-aid. When a member of a dolphin family becomes ill, relatives lift it gently to the surface of the water where it can breathe more easily. The caring cousins also fight off enemies.

Dozing off can be a dangerous business in the ocean. But sea creatures have found ingenious ways to stay safe while they have a quick snooze.

Sweet dreams

Rocky retreat

Despite a giant octopus's huge size, it can wedge itself into a tiny crack. The hole is so small that nothing else can climb in.

Strange but true

Fish have no eyelids. They sleep with their eyes open.

Brain power

It's not easy to fool a dolphin, even if it's fast asleep. When a dolphin takes a nap, half of its brain shuts down. The other half stays wide awake, just in case danger strikes.

▲ An octopus has a lively night-life. During the day it snoozes, but at night it crawls across the ocean floor on the prowl for food.

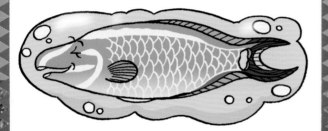

Making the bed

Sea otters always remember to make their own beds. When these furry little creatures settle down for the evening, they snuggle up in a comfortable blanket of giant kelp, which is a type of seaweed. The kelp is rooted to the ocean floor and stops the otters from drifting off in the current.

Hired help

A clownfish has a sea anemone as its personal bodyguard. The clownfish rests comfortably between the anemone's poisonous, waving tentacles, knowing that an enemy will feel a sharp sting if it comes too close!

Ouch! That hurts.

All star aquarium

The seas are packed with superstars. Some are big, others are small, and a few are rare or deadly. But they are all record-breakers.

Big blue

The blue whale is the biggest star of the ocean. This heavyweight is the largest animal ever to have lived in water or on land. It weighs more than 25 elephants.

Killer on the loose

Watch out for the box jellyfish, the most poisonous sea creature. Its body is small, but its tentacles grow up to three metres long. If anything brushes past them, they shoot out tiny poison darts that can kill a human in minutes.

▲ Cats spring into action in the dark. At night, these eagle-eyed creatures hunt for food, play, fight and mate, while other animals are sound asleep.

Eye spy

Night animals don't miss a thing in the dark! Many of these sharp-eyed creatures have huge, bulging eyes to let in as much light as possible. Others peer out through thousands of miniature eyes.

Yikes!

Magical mirrors

Is it a ghost? No, it's just a pair of cat's eyes, shining in the beam of a torch. A layer at the back of each eye reflects the light like a mirror and helps the cat to see in the dark. Big cats in the wild also have eyes that work like mirrors.

68

▲ A tarsier's saucer-like eyes make the most of the dim light. Even when a tarsier is taking a nap, it keeps one eye open for danger.

Open-and-shut case

A gecko licks its eyes to keep them clean! During the day, a gecko protects its sensitive eyes by narrowing the pupils to leave just thin, dark slits. This shuts out most of the blinding sunlight. At night, when the gecko is busy hunting for its dinner, the pupils open wide.

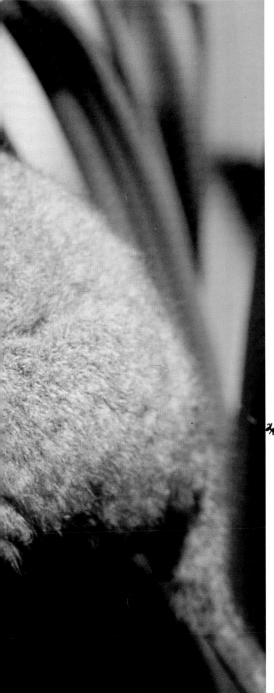

Two-tone vision

Imagine watching a TV with the colour switched off! Anteaters and most other night animals are colour blind, which means they see only in black and white. Also, everything looks blurred, so it helps that they have a good sense of smell and hearing.

Under the microscope

A mosquito is a night-time nibbler that can see in all directions at once. Each eye is made up of thousands of tiny six-sided eyes, which let the mosquito see pictures in many parts, just like a mosaic.

Music to their ears

The night is full of strange noises, from ringing chirps to eerie howls. To us, it means nothing, but to other animals, these sounds are warnings, invitations or just ways to say hello!

What's in a name?

A hyena splits its sides laughing at the sight of a few tasty bones! This cackling creature earns its name from the howling laughter it makes after a successful hunt. When other members of the pack hear the calls, they join the feast.

Beastly suitors

A hammerhead bat is no Prince Charming. Its lips are huge and its cheeks bulge out. But what it lacks in looks, it makes up for in song. Groups of males hang upside down from trees, making ear-splitting honking sounds to attract females. When a female flies past the ugly line-up, she picks the loudest male.

Dangerous call

A male cricket has to pick its partner carefully. It finds a mate by making shrill chirping noises. But the calls also attract the sneaky tachinid fly, which lays eggs on the cricket's body. When the eggs hatch, the young flies eat the cricket.

▲ The chilling howl of a coyote warns other coyotes to keep away.

FROGS MAKE SUCH A RACKET

In spring, the night air around ponds and swamps is thick with croaks, grunts, squeals and whistles. It's the breeding season and romantic male frogs are in fine voice, trying to attract mates.

Hello, gorgeous!

The calls guide female frogs to the breeding place and warn rival males to keep their distance. For the females, it's love at first sight and sound — they hop off towards the croakers of their choice.

71

Tuning in

Most night animals have an excellent sense of hearing. This helps them to hunt for food, avoid the clutches of predators and find their way around in the darkness.

Night-time rustles

A serval on the prowl keeps its ears pricked, listening out for tasty treats. The merest rustle of a juicy mouse sends this wildcat plunging through the long African grass in hot pursuit.

GETTING AN EARFUL!

A bat-eared fox's ears are like huge, curved radio antennae. They pick up even the tiniest night-time sounds.

buzzz

What's that noise?

The flexible ears can turn up, down, left, right and even in two different directions at once!

buzzz

stomp

It's enough to tie your ears in knots.

The fox uses its ears to pinpoint termites, its favourite food. The fox can even hear them in their holes underground.

Sounds like dinner.

stomp   stomp

▼ An aye-aye twitches its bat-like ears as it listens for juicy beetle grubs wriggling inside a branch.

Strange but true

When an aye-aye hears a grub, it bites right through the tree bark. Then it scoops out the struggling insect with its long middle finger.

Who are you calling big ears?

Clickety-click

An oilbird has a special way of avoiding bumps in the night. It makes clicking sounds as it flies. These sounds bounce off trees in its path and return to the bird. By listening to the echoes, this tropical bird judges how close objects are and how to avoid them.

Home, sweet home.

Totally batty

All day long, snoozing bats hang around in caves, trees and attics. But when dusk falls, these airborne acrobats take to the night sky, fluttering their leathery wings.

Hey, move over!

Hook, line and sinker

A fishing bat is an expert night-time hunter. This fierce fighter grabs prize catches from rivers and lakes. The secret of its success is echolocation. The bat makes short, sharp shrieks and listens for the echoes that bounce back off ripples made by fish in the water. Then, it drags its feet through the water until it hooks its slippery prey.

Crowded quarters

Bats live in groups called colonies and often sleep thousands to a roof! A cave in New Mexico, USA, is home to a vast colony of more than 20 million bats. During the day they rest, hanging upside down by their hooked feet.

BAT VERSUS MOTH

Bats love to hunt moths. But the tiger moth knows how to fight back. First, it loops and dives like mad.

I feel sick.

If that fails, the moth makes a loud popping sound. This can startle the bat so much that it gives up the chase.

POP

Was that you?

As a last resort, the moth folds its wings and plummets to the ground. Then it hides until the bat clears off.

Where did he go?

Hairy antics

A scorpion is a nocturnal hairy hazard. When an insect buzzes by, tiny warning bristles on the scorpion's body vibrate. The scorpion quickly grabs the insect with its pincers and stings it with its poisonous tail. Ouch!

Strange but true

A leopard pulls prey equal to its own weight up into the trees with its teeth! Here, its catch is safe from thieving hyenas.

Net trick

A net-throwing spider spends its evenings patiently sitting on a branch. First, it spins a web, which it stretches over its front legs. Then, it waits until an insect walks underneath and drops the net, trapping the creature below.

▲ A leopard crouches in the undergrowth, ready to pounce on its prey. Its spotted coat helps it to blend into the night.

Phantoms

of the night

Few animals are more at home in the dark than owls. These ghostly birds are deadly hunters, with super-sharp eyesight and long-range hearing.

IT'S A HOOT

Cough mixture

Owls eat first and think later! They wolf down mice, voles and other small prey without chewing. But they're not so keen on bones, fur or feathers. So after a while, they cough up the offending bits, bundled into dark pellets.

That's weird

An owl is an amazing contortionist. It can twist its head around to face backwards and even upside-down. When an owl is trying to track down a juicy snack, this acrobatic skill is extremely useful!

Whoo hooo!

Winged phantom

People tell creepy stories of ghostly shapes flitting across moonlit churchyards. The culprits are usually owls which sometimes glow in the dark. The glow is given off by luminous fungi that catch in an owl's feathers after it has rubbed against damp tree bark.

Believe it or not

A barn owl has such fine-tuned hearing that, even high in the air, it can pick up the squeaks and scuffles of mice hidden beneath snow.

▲ This barn owl is swooping silently towards its victim. The owl's feathers are soft, with a fluffy fringe to muffle the sound of its flapping wings.

Family matters

Nocturnal families get together under cover of darkness. Parents have babies and search for new homes, while youngsters play with each other and learn about growing up.

MONSTER EGGS

A nocturnal kiwi lays a jumbo-sized egg. She waddles around for several nights before finally squeezing it out.

Phew! What a whopper! I'm finished.

The male kiwi takes on the tricky job of keeping the huge egg warm until it hatches. This can take up to 85 nights!

This isn't very eggs-citing.

When the chick hatches, it's fully feathered and raring to go. Many other baby birds begin life blind and bare.

I wish I had feathers like that.

Foxy fun and frolics

When young foxes play, it's a mini battlefield. Every evening, these rowdy youngsters, called pups, burst out of their hole to play. Under the watchful eye of their mother, the pups learn vital hunting skills. They play-fight with each other and pounce on anything that moves, from crackling leaves to their parents' tails. Sometimes, an adult throws the pups a live mouse to tease and bully!

Sleepy hide-outs

Honduran white bats snooze the day away under a tent made from large leaves. After a hard night's hunting, they hang upside down, clutching the main vein of a leaf with their clawed feet.

Where's my sleeping bag?

Yippee!

At night, hippos are out and about. But during the hot day, they chill out by wallowing in mud and splashing around in rivers. This lazy pastime helps to protect their skin, which burns easily in the sun.

Phew.

Hippos have another clever way of keeping cool in the heat of the day. Their skin oozes a reddy-pink, oily liquid to stop it from drying out. In the past, this led people to believe that hippos sweated blood!

▲ During the day, a pangolin curls up in its burrow. A predator needs teeth of steel to bite through the pangolin's scaly armour.

Desert life

Most desert animals prefer the night shift, when the hot daytime sun has gone down. They are shade-loving beasts, custom-built to make the most of life among the sand dunes.

I'm out of here!

BOING

Success story

A jerboa is totally unsinkable! At dusk, this sand-dweller pops out of its burrow to feed. It has large toes, which spread out wide to stop it from sinking into the sand. At the first sign of trouble, the beast bounds away like a kangaroo, covering the length of a small car in a single leap.

Clash of the titans

In the ring with a scorpion, a camel-spider is a champion fighter. This nasty night-time spider grows to the size of a saucer, or about 15 centimetres from one leg to another! It dances around the snappy scorpion like a boxer, before leaping in and chewing off the scorpion's poisonous sting.

I win!

What should a fennec fox always keep nearby in the desert? A thirst aid kit!

Believe it or not

During the day, a fennec fox's big ears help it to survive in the hot desert. Heat escapes through the giant ears, helping the fox to cool down.

▲ During the cold desert nights, a fennec fox feels the benefit of a thick fur coat. The fox also has long fur on the soles of its feet to keep it warm and to help it trot easily over the hot sand.

Night-time nightmares

It's spooky in the dark! The strange goings-on of night animals have led to many terrifying tales of make-believe creatures, from swamp monsters to werewolves.

WHO TURNED OFF THE LIGHTS?

Ghastly guzzler

The make-believe stories of Count Dracula are based on the behaviour of real-life vampire bats. These fierce-looking animals sink their razor-sharp fangs into sleeping animals to suck their blood!

SUCKER FOR BLOOD

Dracula is the spine-chilling star of horror stories. At night, the fanged fiend wakes up to guzzle human blood.

Where did I put my fangs?

Quick as a flash, Drac changes into a vampire bat. Then he swoops out of his creepy castle to find a victim.

This is no time to hang around.

When Dracula is about to pounce, he drops his bat disguise. Now, only a cross can scare him off!

Fangs for having me.

90

HALF-MAN...HALF-WOLF...

The CURSE OF THE WEREWOLF

in Eastman COLOR

Believe it or not
According to an ancient legend, only a bullet made from silver can stop a werewolf.

Even the innocent girl who loved him was not safe ...once the full moon rose!

Starring **CLIFFORD EVANS · OLIVER REED · YVONNE ROMAIN · CATHERINE FELLER**
Screenplay by JOHN ELDER · Directed by TERENCE FISHER · Produced by ANTHONY HINDS · Executive Producer MICHAEL CARRERAS
A HAMMER FILM PRODUCTION · A UNIVERSAL-INTERNATIONAL RELEASE

Creature from the black lagoon

Australian legends tell of a blood-curdling, swamp-living monster of the night, called the bunyip. It is said to have flippers like a seal, tusks like a walrus, and a head the shape of an emu. It also has a deafening roar and a taste for human flesh. Yikes!

Look out, I'm back!

91

Night champions

Amazing records abound in the nocturnal world, from aerial acrobats and deafening music-makers to bristly beasts and the ultimate lazy-bones.

Geronimo!

Watch out – it's a flying squirrel! These super-stylish gliders launch themselves off trees at night. Flaps of skin stretch out from the squirrel's arms and legs like wings, turning it into a daredevil hang glider. A flying squirrel would have no problem covering the length of a football pitch in one swoop. Whoosh!

Wonder wings

The Bismark fruit bat is one of the biggest bats of all. This shadowy creature of the night measures a truly terrifying 1.8 metres from wingtip to wingtip. That's almost twice the width of your outstretched arms!

Hello there!

Sharp warning

A North American porcupine bristles with as many as 30,000 spines, making it the prickliest night animal. When this living pin-cushion is threatened, it rattles its quills in warning. As a last resort, it lashes out with its tail, leaving hundreds of quills

Ow! That hurts.

Night song

In many hot countries, the night air rings with the sound of bush crickets. These champion chirpers are among the world's loudest insects. Even if you were sitting in the front of a long train, you could hear a bush cricket chirp from the back end!

SHUT UP!

Slow motion

Yawn! There's no hurrying a sloth. This sleepy-head is one of the world's laziest animals. It snoozes for days on end, hanging securely from a branch by its hook-like claws. When a sloth does stir itself, it crawls incredibly slowly on its belly – standing up takes too much effort! It creeps along at such a snail's pace that moss has time to grow in its hair.

Index